WHO MADE MY LUNCH?

FROM PEANUTS TO PEANUT BUTTER

BY BRIDGET HEOS · ILLUSTRATED BY STEPHANIE FIZER COLEMAN

AMICUS ILLUSTRATED and **AMICUS INK**
are published by Amicus
P.O. Box 1329, Mankato, MN 56002
www.amicuspublishing.us

**LIBRARY OF CONGRESS
CATALOGING-IN-PUBLICATION DATA**
Names: Heos, Bridget, author. | Coleman, Stephanie Fizer, illustrator. | Heos, Bridget. Who made my lunch?
Title: From peanuts to peanut butter : by Bridget Heos ; illustrated by Stephanie Fizer Coleman.
Description: Mankato, MN : Amicus, [2018] | Series: Who made my lunch?
Identifiers: LCCN 2016058341 (print) | LCCN 2017000281 (ebook) | ISBN 9781681511238 (library binding) | ISBN 9781681512136 (ebook) | ISBN 9781681521480 (pbk.)
Subjects: LCSH: Peanut butter—Juvenile literature. | Peanuts—Juvenile literature.
Classification: LCC TP438.P4 H46 2018 (print) | LCC TP438.P4 (ebook) | DDC 664/.8056596—dc23
LC record available at https://lccn.loc.gov/2016058341

EDITOR: Rebecca Glaser
DESIGNER: Kathleen Petelinsek

Printed in China
HC 10 9 8 7 6 5 4 3 2 1
PB 10 9 8 7 6 5 4 3 2 1

ABOUT THE AUTHOR
Bridget Heos is the author of more than 80 books for children. She lives in Kansas City with her husband and four children. Her favorite way to eat peanut butter is with jelly on saltine crackers.

ABOUT THE ILLUSTRATOR
Stephanie Fizer Coleman is an illustrator, tea drinker, and picky eater from West Virginia, where she lives with her husband and two silly dogs. When she's not drawing, she's getting her hands dirty in the garden or making messes in the kitchen.

For a delicious peanut butter sandwich, just twist, spread, and eat! But what if you had to make the peanut butter yourself? And you also had to grow the peanuts?

As a peanut farmer, you'll need to live in a warm climate. Peanuts need about five warm months to grow, so they are grown in the sunny, southern United States.

For seeds, you'll use peanut kernels. No snacking!
You need these to grow more peanuts. Use a tractor
to plant the seeds in long rows. Water and wait.

Where are the peanuts? Peanuts grow underground, but they are not roots. Flowers grow on the peanut plant. Inside each flower is a pod. The pod droops to the ground. Then it pushes underground. There, it becomes a peanut.

Five months later, you can harvest the peanuts. Drive a tractor with a digger attachment up and down the rows. The digger pulls up the peanut plants and shakes off the soil. It lays the plants upside down on the ground.

Let the peanuts dry for a couple days. Then drive a combine, a machine that does a combination of jobs. First, it picks up the plants. Next, it separates the peanuts from the plants.

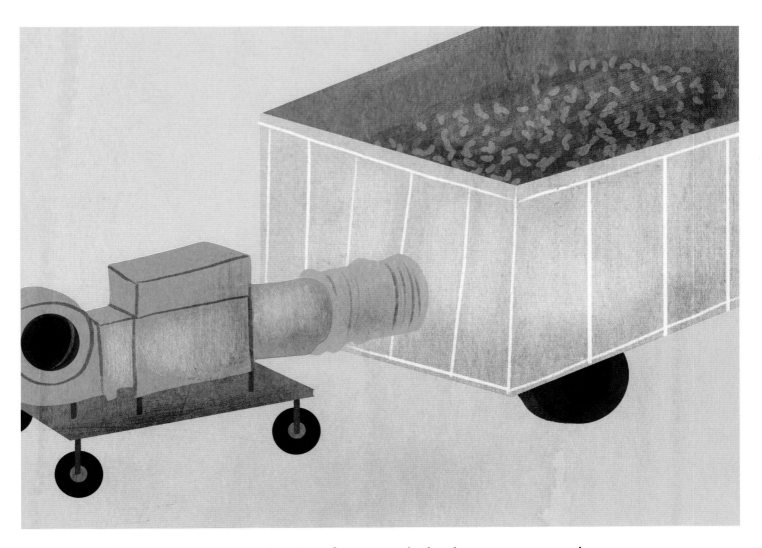

The peanuts will dry for a while longer in a large
peanut wagon with a fan blowing warm air.
Now, the peanuts are trucked to the shelling plant.

Let's crack open those nuts! At the shelling factory, a machine called a sheller pushes the peanuts through grates, removing the shells.

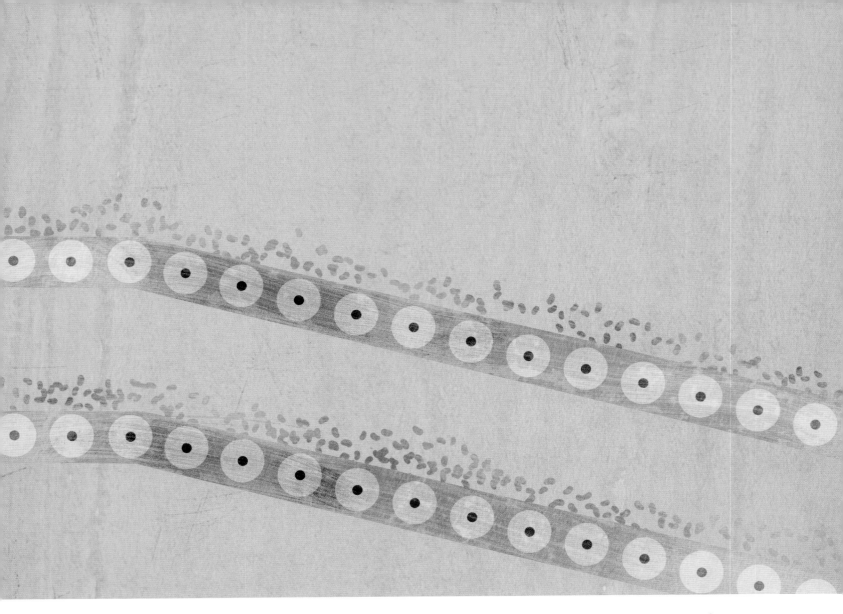

This happens several times until only kernels remain. Put the kernels in big bags and send them to the peanut butter factory.

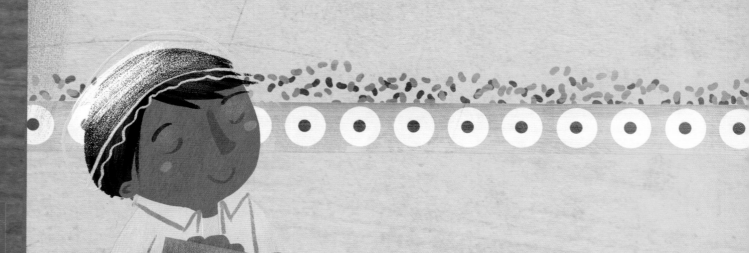

CAUTION!
HOT

At the peanut butter factory, you'll roast the peanuts in a hot oven. The tray moves up and down so that the peanuts shake while they bake. This way, they cook evenly. The white peanuts turn light brown—the color of peanut butter. Mmm . . . smells so good!

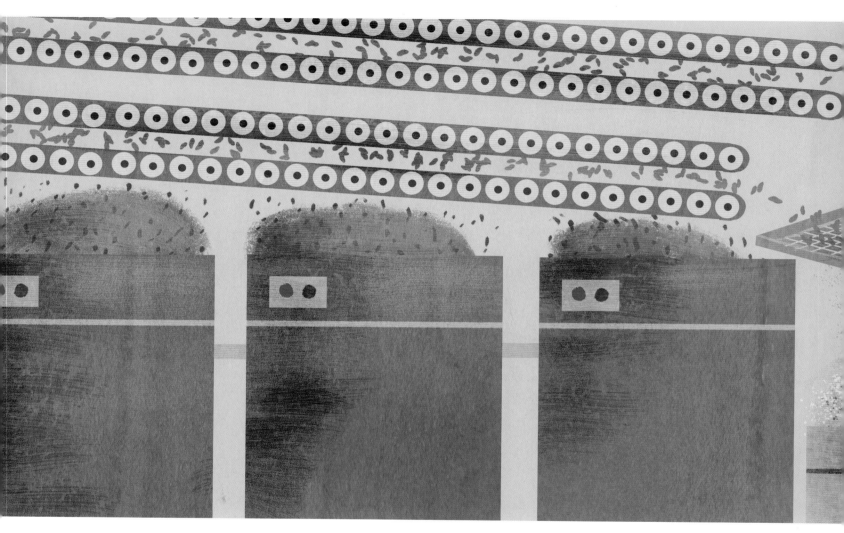

The roasted peanuts move between rubber belts, which removes the skins. Save those! Farmers feed them to their pigs.

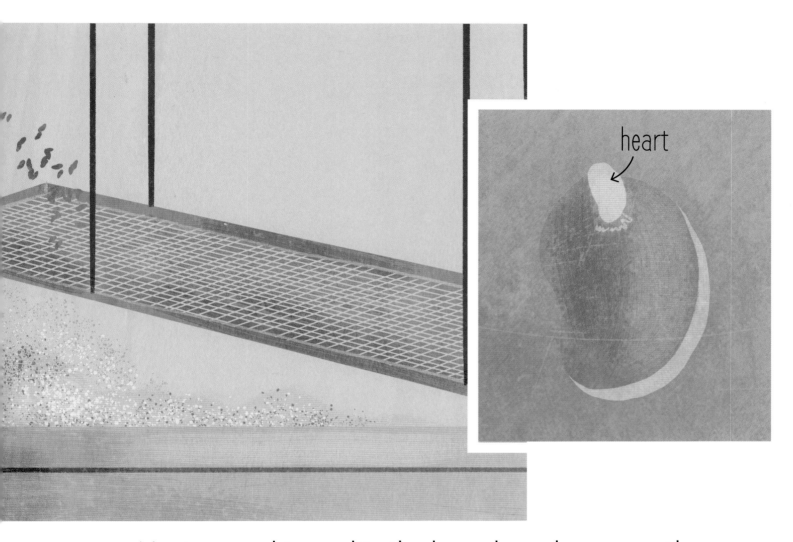

Next, a machine splits the kernels and removes the "heart." That's the tiny lump inside the peanuts. The hearts are a little bitter, but birds love them!

Time to make peanut butter!
Smooth or crunchy?
For crunchy, put most of the
nuts in the grinder, which
grinds them into a smooth
paste. Put the rest in the
chopper, which chops them
into small pieces.

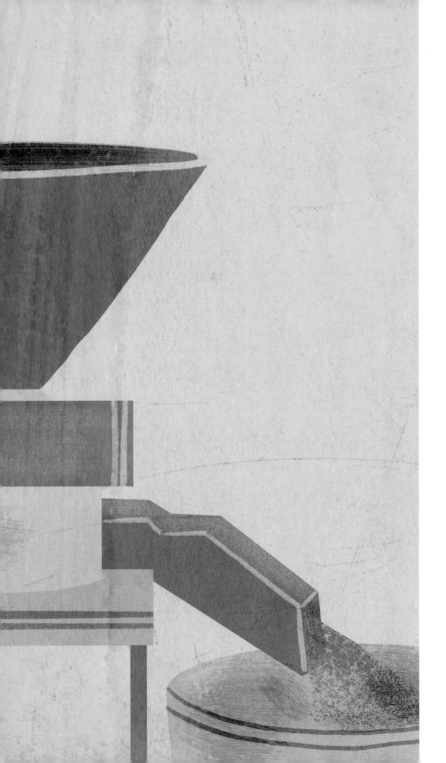

Mix the ground peanuts, chopped peanuts, a little vegetable oil, and salt for flavor. No need to add butter—that's only in the name, not in the actual peanut butter.

For smooth peanut butter, all of the nuts go into the grinder, and no pieces are added. Both types are now put in jars. Squirt!

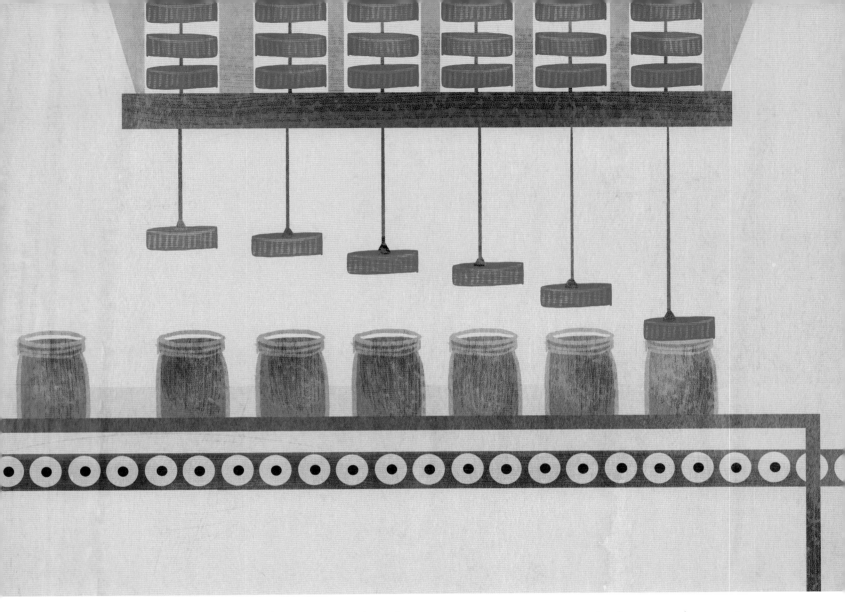

Then another machine seals the jars, screws on lids, and pastes on labels. The peanut butter is off to the grocery store . . .

and onto your sandwich! Thanks to the peanut farmers, shellers, and factory workers, you have a delicious sandwich to eat.

WHERE ARE PEANUTS GROWN?

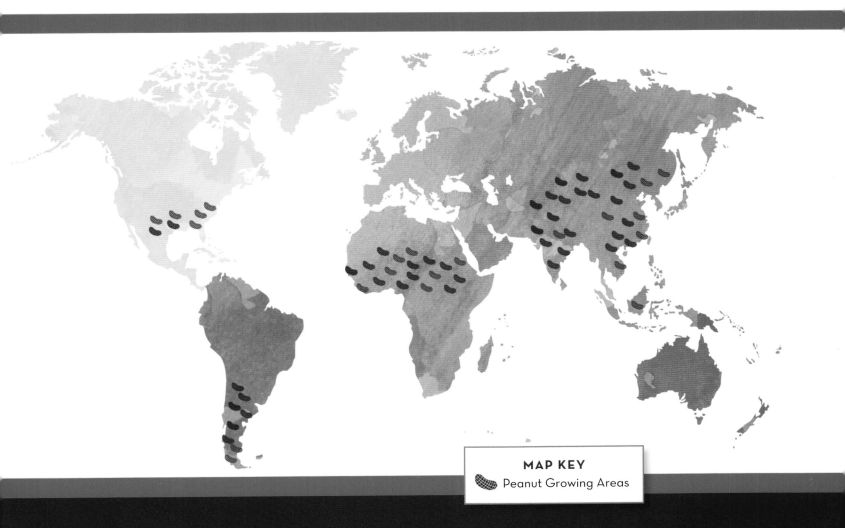

MAP KEY

Peanut Growing Areas

GLOSSARY

combine A machine that does a combination of jobs, separating parts of a plant for harvesting.

digger A machine that digs up peanut plants and lays them in a row.

grinder A machine that crushes something into tiny particles.

kernel The part of a peanut that is able to be eaten.

pod A part of some plants in which seeds grow.

roast To cook at high heat.

shelling plant A building in which nut or peanut shells are removed.

WEBSITES

America's Story from America's Library
http://www.americaslibrary.gov/aa/carver/aa_carver_peanut_1.html
Learn about scientist George Washington Carver's peanut inventions and innovations.

Kids' Health
http://kidshealth.org/en/kids/nut-allergy.html
Learn more about tree nut and peanut allergies.

Nourish Interactive
http://www.nourishinteractive.com/kids
Solusville: A Healthy Neighborhood. Games related to healthy eating.

Every effort has been made to ensure that these websites are appropriate for children. However, because of the nature of the Internet, it is impossible to guarantee that these sites will remain active indefinitely or that their contents will not be altered.

READ MORE

Bailey, R.J. *Peanut Butter.* Minneapolis: Jump!, Inc., 2016.

Bernard, Jan and John Willis. *Peanut Butter.* New York, NY: AV2 by Weigl, 2017.

Nolan, Janet. *PB&J Hooray!: Your Sandwich's Amazing Journey from Farm to Table.* Chicago: Albert Whitman & Co., 2014.